CW00494255

Two Weeks Notice To Quit Your Job And Become Your Own Boss:

Be Successful, And Enjoy Financial Flexibility

By

Amanda porter

Table of content

Introduction

You've put in years of endless effort at jobs that left you bored, uninspired, and unfulfilled. You're ready for a transition. You desire control over your destiny. You want to be in charge of your schedule and work on a project that you are deeply engaged in. You desire and wish to work for yourself. But how do you recognize this dream? You might believe you have a skill set that you might use to create a successful business or that you have a wonderful business idea. This manual will assist you in achieving your goals and improving your existing circumstances as you work toward being your boss.

Chapter 1

How to make your Dreams come true

The best time to start living your goals is present. If you put in the work and create a practical plan, you can achieve your goals. Knowing what you want and taking tiny measures will put you on the road to success. Of course, there are difficulties on the way, but if you focus on learning from your failures, you will succeed in achieving your goals. Would you like to know how to achieve these goals? refer to the Steps.

1-make your dream become a burning desire.

You will need to transform your dream into a fierce desire. A strong desire to realize your goals can give you more self-assurance and help you get through some of the most trying times in life. Believing that your objective is attainable and that you can truly accomplish it will help change it from a pipe dream into a strong desire. If you only see it as a broad desire, like wanting to lose five pounds this year, You won't be able to take it seriously if it's only a wish to relocate somewhere sunny. You should stop referring to something as a dream once a burning desire develops because a dream by definition implies that it is not real. You must begin to consider it as something more. It's important to change from a dream to an intense desire, and then to a goal.

3-Make your burning desires become goals.

The next step is to turn your deep desire into a goal. Because you are confident in your ability to succeed, you earlier turned your aspiration into a fierce desire. You must, however, have faith in your ability to carry it through if you want to make it a goal. This type of belief is predicated on your conviction that, if it can be done, you can do it, and that, if you can do it, you can do it right this second. The issue with goals is that they require time. establishing a deadline makes it easier for you to commit to accomplishing something sensitive. After you've made your deepest desire into a goal, you can no longer refer to it as a deep wish or a dream; it is now your life's purpose and something you must accomplish.

4-Create a Plan.

Create a well-thought-out action plan. To achieve your goals, you will need to develop a strategy. This strategy is typically referred to as a plan or an action plan. There isn't a single course of action that works for everyone because each strategy depends on the individual and the objectives they hope to achieve. As a result, you must look within yourself for the answers necessary to develop your effective course of action. Detail each phase of your plan in writing. Putting it in writing can help you feel more realistic and attainable. Just keep in mind that life isn't always clear-cut, and you might not be able to neatly cross off one goal after another. You might also decide to change some of the necessary steps for realizing your dreams or come up with a new route along the way.

5-execute your plan

Following the creation of a personalized action plan based on your goals, you must take initiative and seize any chance that presents itself. It's time to quit putting off until tomorrow what may be done now and to stop creating excuses. There are many good reasons to postpone fulfilling your aspirations, such as having to prepare for your wedding, experiencing a hectic period at work, becoming involved in a difficult relationship, etc., but if you adopt this mentality, you'll never achieve your goals. You risk spending an eternity coming up with reasons why you can't accomplish something. Like attracts like, and when there is a need, the universe seems to find a way to fill it through chances, according to the law of attraction. When you move forward with your plans to accomplish your goals, which will help you fulfill your deepest desire and realize your dream, you must be ready for them.

7-Always Review your progress

It's crucial to have an understanding of your progress when you set out on the road to realizing your dreams. Rome wasn't built in a day, and you might not be moving forward as rapidly as you'd want, but it's still crucial to feel like you are. When producing your personal progress report, take note of the following:

-If your rules are met for that time frame.

-If you still want to achieve your dreams.

-If you have strayed from the path leading to the achievement of your goal.

Chapter 2

How to give notice to your boss

What's the best approach to giving your employer notice that you're quitting? If you leave on good terms, you will have a better chance of obtaining a favorable work reference

Do provide **notice** when you can. It is customary to give two weeks' notice when resigning unless the situation is intolerable. You might resign suddenly for several reasons, such as if you feel threatened or are being harassed sexually. It is acceptable to ask whether you can go immediately if those reasons don't apply to your current circumstance. Even though you know you've given your notice at work, you could still feel anxious about making the proper choice in departing. The most crucial aspect of giving notice is leaving politely, regardless of whether you're doing so because you've accepted a new position, in which case congratulations are due, or because your circumstances have changed. You should be straightforward with your manager while giving your notice, express your appreciation for the organization, and try not to cross any bridges.

1. Allow your boss to know before anyone else

Making sure your supervisor doesn't say "I know" when you ultimately give your notice is one of the most crucial components of providing notice. Even though you might be itching to tell your fifty closest coworkers about your new position or your plans to quit, you should wait until your supervisor is aware of the situation before sharing any information with your family. In order to show your boss respect and to act professionally, you should do this. Also, never talk about it on social media. Before the rest of the world learns, make sure your boss and coworkers do.

2. Do it yourself.

Unless you and your boss reside in very different regions of the country, you owe it to your supervisor to arrange a meeting to discuss your impending departure. You should make the effort to speak with your supervisor face-to-face rather than writing a letter or sending an email, even if you don't get along with them well or you have some hatred toward them. This conveys the idea that you value your work and want to put forth the time and effort necessary to do so.

4. Ensure you do have a transition plan

Your manager will inquire about your work-related plans after you give notice. You should have a plan for how to complete the projects you were working on, delegate tasks, explain any systems you may have implemented, transition existing clients, and do whatever else necessary to make sure the business continues to run successfully without you. This might help the scenario feel more upbeat and will impress your supervisor. Also, it will demonstrate your thoughtful consideration and concern for the company's future.

5 .you can leave on the same day if necessary

Having a transition plan is a good idea, but you can run into an irate supervisor who wants you to quit immediately now. You need to be ready to pack up your belongings as soon as possible if this is the case. While you shouldn't pack your office before speaking with your supervisor, you should be sure to gather any crucial documents in case you are asked to leave right away. Although it doesn't happen frequently, it could be if your employer becomes upset or irritated. Just in case, be ready for it so you'll know what to do next.

Chapter 3

How to prepare yourself for success

Although there isn't a certain recipe for success, you can prepare yourself more effectively to develop one.

Important Reminder

There are plenty of pre-made success tactics available. But any recipe for achievement needs to be customized, starting with your values and life objectives. Here are five suggestions for improving your pre-trip preparation. The majority of people aspire to success. It's a strong psychological motivator because we find self-worth in our accomplishments and because society values them. We're enamored with the idea, and no CEO, celebrity, businessperson, or even marginally famous YouTuber seems to be able to hold a conversation without someone enquiring as to "What's the key to your success?" Everybody who wants to succeed must develop a formula based on their particular objectives and circumstances. However, there are a wide variety of success factors available to you that are not all connected to your job or financial situation. You can find fulfillment in your relationships, charitable work, physical wellness, and even your sense of self-affection.

Here are five things to think about as you get ready for success.

1. Begin with your values, not your goals

The first pitfall to avoid is thinking that to succeed, you must excel in everything. You'll rapidly find yourself handling too much if you try to handle everything without focusing on doing it correctly. It is where the madness, stress, and lack of time are. Before you even begin, you'll feel overpowered. Start with your values and use them to find the successes that resonate with you to avoid overloading yourself. "Don't spend a stressful amount of time evaluating the significance of each objective and activity. Starting with why we're going to do something is better than what we're going to do. So, we ought to start with our principles. begin by classifying your values into three areas of your life: your relationships, your career, and yourself. Finally, use these principles as a guide to decide where to focus your attention, what objectives you want to achieve, and how much time you should devote to each objective. Contemplate working out. Your well-being is important. There are no questions. Sadly, when their fad-like, over-hyped, and unsustainable fitness plans don't deliver optimal results in the promised 6 weeks or less, consumers might frequently feel like failures.

But do bodybuilder-like gains that are ready to appear on glossy covers have any bearing on your health, relationships, career, or sense of worth? If not, why spend effort trying to find them? Set attainable objectives that will make you happy and healthy and are focused on the types of activity and way of life you value.

2. Do not implement without understanding

Another mental mistake is to assume you know what success entails and to start pursuing it right away. It's best to concentrate on learning the ropes rather than diving right in. give it some thought, then plan how you'll participate. This approach applies to other ambitions as well, such as mastering a second language, a musical instrument, or the nuances of indoor gardening, even though you might not be making a transition into a leadership position. But there is a condition. Some people risk over-preparing themselves throughout the planning process, never starting to work toward their goals.

3. generate early momentum and small wins

The required modifications may at times seem excessive. You can find the process scary or impractical because there are so many steps between you and your final objective.

But no matter how little the win, success breeds success. This is why you should build on your minor victories to achieve bigger ones. Even if those early successes are actually about enhancing your credit or being perceived as an integral part of the organization, you need to be looking for opportunities to achieve some early wins. AnotherThe best strategy is to take your big goals, break them down into manageable chunks, and work on each one separately. You'll be more likely to start and complete smaller tasks since they're more realistic and less daunting. As a result, you start to feel more confident about your capacity to achieve, and each success turns into a milestone you can exploit to advance even further.

4. Create a network

Using your network or, if none already exists for you, starting to create them as part of your goals are other ways to gain momentum. As you start to go forward with those crucial early initiatives that are going to create momentum for you, you need to be thinking in terms of the essential relationships that you need to make and the alliances that you need to create. Another justification for collaboration Is, it gives your success greater significance. Relationships can be developed and strengthened by giving and receiving assistance because it fosters a sense of community and, ultimately, shared success. A continual search for improvement is what keeps us alive and what keeps us actively engaged.

5. establishing success through failure

We are frequently exposed to other people's successes on TV, in newsletters, and in our social media feeds, even if we may rationally realize that any accomplishment includes failures built into the foundation. And by the time those get to us, their mistakes have already become history while ours are anything but.

Chapter 4

How to describe your startup idea.

Your proposal must be clearly and attention-grabbingly described for it to be effective. It must cause people to exclaim, "Aha!, that's interesting." More, please.

This is an example:

The One-Sentence Pitch Format from The Founder Institute (one sentence)

business name

is evolving (a defined offering)

in order (a target audience)

(Fix a situation)

(with a hidden ingredient)

For instance, my business, the Founder Institute, is creating a mentoring and training program to assist entrepreneurs in learning new startups and building lasting technology companies with shared equity that promotes peer support.

By giving (advantage), we can overcome problems and assist (target) in achieving (target's aim).

You might next add another phrase outlining your company concept, depending on the stage you've reached:

By charging clients to receive benefits, we earn money.

By giving employees access to a live feed of comments and queries, for instance, we help businesses become more productive. We charge businesses who desire administrative control over their employee networks to make money.

Answer these questions by describing your ideas.

What issue do you hope to resolve?

Who encounters that issue?

How do you intend to resolve that issue?

Why this is a superior approach

As an illustration, I want to address the issue of clean water scarcity in developing nations. Those who live in rural areas without adequate infrastructure for water delivery and treatment are affected by this issue. I intend to provide village-scale pumps that would enable every hamlet to access clean water from underground sources to address that issue. This would be a preferable option because it would be quick and simple to install, simple to use, wouldn't need significant infrastructure investments, and would last. even sell clean water to make money for rural business owners.

Always choose your words carefully while describing your startup idea and test it with prospective clients and investors.

Chapter 5

know and identify your ideal customer profile

What exactly is a client profile?

First and foremost, we must define "client profile." A customer profile is just a description of a specific sort of customer. Your ideal customer profile (ICP) should provide you with basic information on the ideal users of your service. This can comprise a wide range of client attributes, such as demographics such as age, business objective, and geographical area, as well as more personal variables such as interests, lifestyle, and family, among others.

5 stages to defining your ideal customer profile.

These are five basic actions you can take to determine your ideal consumer profile and begin developing an effective marketing strategy.

1. Know the problem your business solves.

You presumably already know what problem your company can solve for customers. Make sure you understand why your company can assist customers in resolving a specific issue. Marketing typically focuses on articulating what problem your firm can answer, as this can assist you more simply define which consumers may be experiencing this difficulty in the first place. This should always be the initial step in defining an ICP. Once you've determined your answer, you'll have a good idea of the types of customers that are likely to benefit from and purchase your business.

2. Investigate and find your top customers.

If your company is already up and operating, follow the lead of your most dependable returning clients. Analyse demographics and research utilizing website traffic, ad interaction, and sales analytics. Search for patterns. Are all of your best customers, for example, over the age of 30? This could be an indication that your marketing should target this age group. Perhaps your consumers are primarily from Europe. Knowing your current consumer demographics will assist you in reevaluating your first instincts about your ICP. In other circumstances, the statistics may astound you, and you may end up with a different ICP than you expected.

3. Evaluate both positive and negative customer comments.

Data is an important part of creating an ideal client profile, but it should not be your exclusive source of information. Strive to get to know your consumers on a more intimate level as well. Arrange phone calls or in-person meetings with your greatest clients if possible to learn why they adore your business. This one-on-one contact can help you discover aspects of your ICP that data may not have revealed.

4. Define key customer traits.

Compile your findings after conducting your study and analysis. Now is the time to put pen to paper and build a written customer profile. Every company's list of characteristics will be slightly different, however, the basic ICP should include information about the:

Location geographically

Age group

Size of the business

Software budget or annual revenue

Location

A good ICP will also provide answers to more subtle and contextual questions regarding the desired organization. In this Harvard Business School case study, you can see the value of employing a complicated segmentation strategy that integrates data based on attitudes and behavioral patterns, such as: What are the company's major challenges?

What technology are they currently employing?

How long has the company been in business?

What are their annoyances?

What objectives do they consider?

What are the core values of their brand?

You might even think about integrating more personal characteristics, especially if there is a pattern in your present customer base, such as:

Gender of the employee

Lifestyle\sHobbies

Family relationships

You might also evaluate negative characteristics or characteristics of consumers who have proven to be a poor fit for your software. This will save you money on marketing that actively seeks out weak prospects.

5. Utilize your ICP to improve your brand and marketing approach

Once you've created a clear image of your ideal customer profile, you can utilize it to specifically target the correct companies in your marketing campaigns. The first step is to identify who your ideal consumers are. The more information you have about them, the easier it will be to find and promote them.

6. Identifying Ideal Customers

Who do you believe your target audience is? The easiest way to find your ideal customers is to construct a buyer or customer persona, which is a fictional portrayal of them. The important thing is to be as specific as possible. If you're already in business, you could already know something about them. Begin with your current consumer base; they will provide the most information.

8. Developing Consumer Personas

Create your profiles when you've gathered all of your client persona data. Here's an example of a bicycle retailer's consumer persona:

David is a 55-year-old professional with a $190,000 household income. He is married with children and lives in the suburbs. He is concerned about fitness and spends $10,000-$20,000 each year on jewelry and accessories. He desires functional, high-quality items that reflect prestige.

You may need to build many client personas depending on the type of business you own, what you sell, and how many customers you have. Don't let this overwhelm you; start with your most valuable consumers and construct simply a few personalities. You can always make more afterward.

9. Professionals who are too sophisticated for your product or service

Students that are only interested in your content for academic purposes

Prospective clients who are simply too costly to acquire due to a low average sale price or a high attrition rate, locating more Ideal Clients.

Design your marketing and sales strategy to attract your ideal clients using your customer profiles by:

-Advertising in the medium where they spend the majority of their time

(online, blogs, websites, print, TV, radio)

-Developing marketing and advertising messaging that address their problems.

-Using social media to share relevant content to their problems

Use their words and phrases in your sales and marketing material.

Using their favorite method of communication (text, visual, video, long-form, short-form)

Concentrate your sales efforts on your preferred consumers by:

-Purchasing prospect lists that match your ideal customer profile

-Using social media to target people who fit your desired consumer profile

-Obtaining referrals from your ideal clients

-Selling your goods or service through their chosen means of distribution

-Determining your ideal customers will assist you in weeding out less-than-perfect customers.

Those who are more difficult to sell spend less money and are less profitable. By concentrating on your ideal consumers and figuring out the best approach to communicate with them, your company will expand faster and more profitably.

Chapter 6

How to generate more subscribers with a lead magnet

Do you want to increase your subscriber base? If this is the case, you must design a high-quality lead magnet to convince your audience to subscribe to you. Lead Magnets are freebies that you will present to your subscribers in exchange for their email addresses or add them to your email lists. It is a method of encouraging your subscribers to remain loyal to your brand. The goal of lead magnets is to turn your existing customers into loyal audiences or subscribers. Generally, lead magnets are generated using ebooks or micro ebooks, however, this is insufficient for some users because not everyone enjoys reading. It takes time to read, and it takes time to produce. What are some creative ways to generate lead magnets to gain more subscribers?

1. List of Resources

A resource list is an excellent concept for a lead magnet. It is usually a collection of articles, websites, tools, and other resources that you want to include. The resource list is a big aid to scholars because they can just click on the link. Remember not to just add the links, convert it to PDF, and then leave it alone. Consider a novel approach to creating a resource so that your subscribers believe they are obtaining a high-quality lead magnet.

2.PDF

PDF Version is the most effective lead magnet of all. Convert your blog post directly to PDF and make it available for download on your website. This lead magnet is beneficial to your blog readers since they can read your blogs after downloading the pdf without needing to connect to the internet at any time.

3. Checklist

Developing a checklist is the simplest and quickest lead magnet, and it works in a variety of industries. For example, if you offer skin care goods, you might start a blog about skincare and establish a checklist of the products that must be utilized to attain healthy skin. The list of requirements that you produced is available for free download by signing up for their emails. Most people find the checklist simple to use. They can utilize it immediately after downloading it.

5. Making Use of a Facebook Group

We are all aware that Facebook is currently the most influential platform. If creating a membership site is difficult for you, consider using a closed Facebook group that your subscribers may enter by supplying their email addresses. As a lead magnet, Facebook Group needs you to put in more effort to engage your Facebook group members; you must publish insightful content to keep your members entertained and be active in communicating with other members.

6. Template

Templates are one of the more interesting lead magnets you can provide. As a blogger, you can build a downloadable template that your subscribers can use. For example, if you're a well-known blogger, you can design one-of-a-kind themes to post on their social media accounts. Templates can also be utilized in a variety of sectors. For example, establishing a template for resumes, biodata, and time sheets. Users can benefit from templates because they can simply download them and begin filling out the essential information.

Chapter 7
How to increase followers on your social media.

Small businesses must now be online with a website and on social media with many profiles. Why? Because that is where your audience, and thus your consumers and clients, are.Why is it necessary to boost your social media followers? The more followers you have, the more people will be aware of your fantastic business. Those who follow you do so because they like what you do or give. Converting purchases is considerably easier when your audience is already interested in learning more. Hence, here are eight tried-and-true small company methods for increasing social media followers:

1. Your brand should be one that people want to follow.

This may seem obvious, but you'd be amazed at how many people believe that simply being 'out there' is enough to garner followers. Tease your viewers with stuff that will entice them to click. Consider the brands you support and why. Your brand account must have material that draws the attention of a potential follower and plenty of things to like and share. Make sure your profile is complete to provide substance and legitimacy. Give your brand a backstory and personalize it. Place your photograph prominently.

2. Search for and follow other brands and influencers who share your vision.

Don't do it in the hopes of receiving a follow back. Do it because their fans may start following you back. If you want your brand to be real, you should interact favorably with the people and brands that represent it. Like things that speak to you, share stuff that you believe your followers would enjoy, and leave comments whenever possible. People will be intrigued by you and will follow you.

3. Allow your material to be easily discovered.

Some folks are Instagram addicts, others are Facebook addicts, some are Twitter addicts on their breaks, and some are LinkedIn junkies during the week. Therefore share your content with others. Someone may find you on Facebook and then follow you on Instagram because they enjoy your images, or they may see your LinkedIn company page and decide to follow your Twitter handle. Cast a wide net and post on all platforms, ensuring sure your social media profiles are on each one. That will give you the finest opportunity to gain new followers.

4. Always post, but don't spam.

If you just post once in a while, you soon become irrelevant, and followers don't need many reasons to unfollow you when they have so many options.

There are no hard and fast rules, but instead follow the natural flow of each network, thus for example, Twitter and Instagram churn over content quickly, whereas Facebook and LinkedIn are a little slower and articles can sit for a while. Scheduling is a terrific method to keep your social channels active, so give it a shot!

Several social media management systems include automatic reminders to help you publish on a regular basis. Find out more about how and when you are pressed for time, and keep active on social media. In addition to scheduling, you may set up a repeating posts system, which will save you a lot of time. You can schedule specific static postings, such as events or happy hours, to be automatically repeated so you don't have to think about scheduling or posting them separately for months or even the rest of the year. Publish on a regular basis but avoid spamming.

7. Interact with your audience

Remember when having direct access to a global superstar via Twitter was exciting and revolutionary? It was amazing to be able to write them a note or directly hear what a Hollywood celebrity had to say. Consumers want to connect with the person behind a brand. They want to hear what you have to say, and revealing yourself to your audience develops trust. Thus, respond to comments, remarks, and inquiries. Isn't that the joy of social media?

8. Utilize advertising

For most small businesses, advertising is a terrific strategy to gain a large number of followers. You should not be scared to use ads to gain followers, especially when you are just starting. Advertising, on the other hand, does not produce cost-effective results unless it is effectively targeted. The simplest method for a local business is to target ads locally. The majority of social platforms feature well-guided and predefined "follower acquisition" strategies. Do not hesitate to commit a tiny amount to create your follower base since it will pay off later for sure! If you've been neglecting your social media, use these tried-and-true strategies to increase your followers and brand immediately.

Printed in Great Britain
by Amazon